A FUN AND EASY WAY TO
CLEAN YOUR ROOM

Written By Joy Berry
Illustrated by Bartholomew

Joy Berry Enterprises, Inc.
146 West 29th St., Suite 11RW
New York, NY 10001

Cover Design & Art Direction: John Bellaud
Art Production: Geoff Glisson
All music remastered at Midtown Sound Studios NYC, 2008

Printed in Mexico

ISBN 978-1-60577-312-4

This is a fun and easy book about cleaning your room. This book tells you what you need to know about
- making your bed,
- picking up whatever is out of place,
- putting things away,
- dusting the furniture,
- cleaning the floor,
- putting away cleaning supplies,
- organizing your things.

How do you feel when you need to clean your room?

Do you sometimes feel overwhelmed and frustrated?

When you need to clean your bedroom, do you wonder…

If you follow the instructions outlined in this book, you can clean your room, no matter how messy or dirty it is!

The first thing you need to do is to **clear everything off your bed.**

If your sheets need changing, now is the time to remove the dirty sheets and replace them with clean ones.

Follow these steps to make your bed look neat and feel comfortable:

Step 1: Begin at the head of the bed. Slip the corners of the bottom sheet over the corners of the mattress. Most bottom sheets have fitted corners.

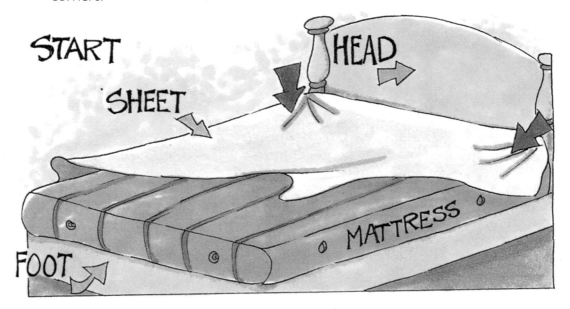

Step 2: Do the same thing at the foot of the bed. Lifting the mattress corners as you slip the sheet over them will make the job easier.

Step 3: Put the top sheet on the bed. Place the wide hem of the sheet at the head of the bed. Check to see that the top sheet hangs down evenly on both sides of the bed. Also, remember to place the top sheet face down on the bed so that the decorative side of the sheet shows when it is folded back over the blanket.

Step 4: Spread the blanket (or blankets) on top of the sheets. Place one end of the blanket about 8 inches down from the head of the mattress. Check to see that the blanket hangs down evenly on both sides of the bed.

Step 5: Fold the top sheet back over the edge of the blanket at the head of the bed.

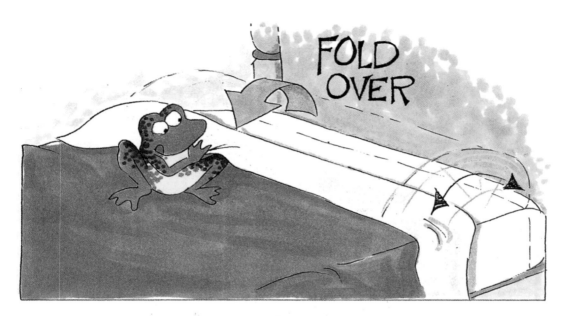

Step 6: Tuck the ends of the sheet and the blanket under the mattress at the foot of the bed.

Step 7: Finish off the corners at the foot of the bed one at a time. Pick up the side edges of the sheet and the blanket approximately 12 inches from the foot of the bed. Fold these edges over the top of the mattress. Tuck the remaining part of the sheets and the blanket under the mattress.

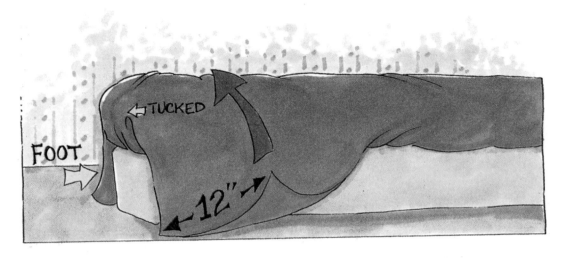

Step 8: Pick up the edges of the sheet and the blanket that you folded back and tuck these under the mattress. Tuck in the sheet and the blanket that is hanging over the sides of the bed.

Step 9: Now put your bedspread on top of the bed. Check to see that the bedspread hangs evenly all around the bed. The edges should barely touch the floor. Fold back about 20 inches of the spread at the head of the bed.

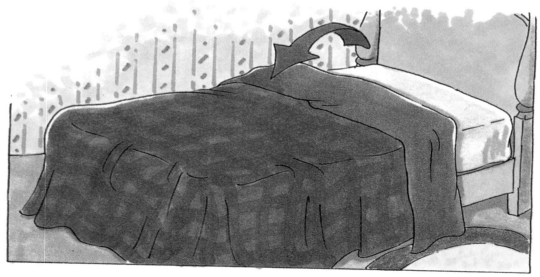

Step 10: Put clean pillow cases on your pillows, and place them at the head of the bed. Pull the bedspread up over the pillow and tuck the edge of the bedspread behind the pillow.

After your bed is made, **pick up whatever is out of place and put it on your bed.**

Use your bed to hold the things that you pick up until you can put them where they belong.

To make sure that you don't miss anything, begin picking up in the area to the left side of your bedroom door and work around the entire room.

Now, **put away the things that are on your bed.** Pick up one item at a time, and decide where it belongs. Once you pick up something, put it away. Do not set it back on the bed.

Put things exactly where they belong. It is important to put them away neatly. Do not stuff things just anywhere, simply to get them out of sight.

If you pick up something that needs to be thrown away, put it into a large paper sack or plastic trash bag.

If you pick up an article of dirty clothing, put it in a "dirty clothes" pile outside of your bedroom door.

If you pick up some clean clothing, carefully put it away where it belongs.

Hang blouses, shirts, jackets, coats, and dresses on hangers.

Button the top button or zip up the zipper so that the clothing will not slide off the hanger.

Hang skirts on skirt hangers or fasten them to regular hangers with safety pins.

Hang pants by the cuffs on a pants hanger or drape them over the bottom of a regular hanger so that the pants hang evenly on both sides. Pants should be smoothed out, with the crease running down the middle of the leg.

Some articles of clothing need to be properly folded before you put them away. To fold underwear and shorts, smooth them out and fold them in half. Match socks and fold each pair in half or in thirds. If you want your socks to stay up when you wear them, don't stretch the cuffs back down over the socks when you fold them. Belts should be rolled up or hung up.

To fold a T-shirt, knit top, or sweater, spread it out with the front face down. Fold back an equal amount on each side, and fold the sleeves down. Fold the bottom up, and carefully turn the clothing over. This is how it will look when you are through.

After you have put everything where it belongs, **dust the furniture in your room.** Begin with the furniture to the left of your bedroom door, and work around the entire room. You can use a feather duster to brush the dust off of an object. Use a cloth with a small amount of furniture polish on it to pick up the dust.

When you dust something, first dust the top of the object, then the sides, and then the bottom.

When you have finished dusting all of the furniture, **vacuum, sweep or dust the floor of your room.** Remember to begin with the area to the left of your bedroom door, and work your way around the room.

Make sure that you get under and behind your bed and the other furniture.

To **finish** the job, you need to put away all of the cleaning supplies carefully.

- Put away the dust cloth, feather duster, furniture polish, vacuum cleaner, broom and dust mop.

- Take the pile of dirty clothes to wherever the dirty laundry is kept.
- Put the trash from your room into the trash can.

If you had trouble deciding where to put the things on your bed, you may need to **get your room organized** so that everything has a place.

If you decide to organize your room, follow these two suggestions:

#1 Begin with a clean room.

If you begin with a disorderly room, you will be faced with a big mess when you start emptying your shelves and drawers. This can frustrate you and make you want to quit before the job is done.

#2 Work on one small area at a time.

If you empty all your shelves and drawers at the same time, you will create a pile of clutter that is overwhelming. That might cause you to do a sloppy job just to get it over with.

To help you to organize your room, follow this plan:

Get three boxes with lids that can be closed.

- Label one box **Toss.**
- Label the second box **Recycle.**
- Label the third box **Hold.**

Gather some containers to store things in.

Here is what you need:

- shoe boxes and containers with plastic lids,
- medium-sized boxes, preferably ones with lids (available at most stores), and
- plastic storage bags in several sizes.

Decide where you want to put things.

You will need to choose a shelf, a drawer, or a special area for each of these groups of things:

- books, magazines, and comic books,
- art and craft supplies,
- stationery (paper, pens, pencils, and erasers),
- school supplies,
- hobbies and collections,
- toys and games,
- sports and recreation equipment,
- musical instruments,
- clothes that need to be hung up,
- clothes that need to be folded,
- shoes and boots,
- personal care items (combs and brushes), and
- photographs, souvenirs, and keepsakes

Put the contents of one shelf, one drawer, or the closet on your bed.

Put away the things on your bed.

Pick up one object at a time, and decide where to put it. Once you have picked up something, put it away. Do not set it back down.

You might decide that an article you pick up is of no use to anyone because it is broken, beyond repair, or used up. Put it in the box marked **Toss.**

You might decide that an object you pick up is in good working condition but that you don't want it anymore. Put it in the box marked **Recycle.**

If you're not sure about what to do with an article that you pick up (for example, something that you haven't used in a long time but that you might want to keep), put it in the box marked **Hold.**

If you pick up an object that you know you frequently use and want to keep, carefully put it away in the special place that you have chosen for it.

Here are some tips to help you as you put things away:

- Anything smaller than a golf ball (game parts, doll accessories, pieces of models) should be stored in small plastic bags.
- Anything that is about the size of a baseball should be stored with other items of similar size in shoe boxes and cans.
- Store all of the items in one group together in a box, in a drawer, or in your closet.
- Label your drawers, shelves, and containers so that you or anyone else will know where to put things.
- Label your things so that they can be returned to you easily if they are ever misplaced.
- Get rid of worn-out or outgrown items before you put any new ones away. This saves you from digging through a pile of old things to get to the new ones.

Here are some suggestions for organizing your clothes:

- Group your clothes according to a plan. You may want to put all of your shirts or blouses together, all of your pants together, and so on. Or you may want to put all of your play clothes together and all of your dressy clothes together. Having a plan will help you to find things more easily when you are getting dressed.
- Put freshly laundered clothes at the bottom of your drawers and take what you need from the top of the stack. This way, everything gets used and you don't end up wearing the same things again and again.

After you have organized all of your things, put everything that is in the box marked **Toss** into the trash.

Make a plan for getting rid of the things in the **Recycle** box.
These items can be
- given to a friend,
- traded for something else,
- sold, or
- given to a non-profit organization that recycles used items.

Get rid of everything in the box right away so that the items for recycling don't get mixed in with your other things.

Store the box marked **Hold.**

Write the date on the **Hold** box, close it up, and put it in a safe, dry place. If you don't need the things in the box during the next year, the chances are that you will never need them. After a year, you should put them in the **Recycle** box the next time you organize your things.

Once your room is clean and organized, keeping it that way is easier if you

- keep a wastebasket in your room to hold your trash,
- keep a hamper for dirty clothes in your room,
- straighten up your room every day,
- clean your room once a week, and
- organize your things at least twice a year.

Remember, a clean room is worth the time and effort that you spend to get it that way.